Instrumental Solos
By Special Arrangement

Eleven Songs Arranged in a Jazz Style with Written-Out Improvisations

Arranged by Carl Strommen

CONTENTS

Recording producer: Greg Minnick, Levelblu Music Productions.

GERSHWIN® and GEORGE GERSHWIN® are registered trademarks of Gershwin Enterprises
IRA GERSHWIN® is a trademark of Gershwin Enterprises
PORGY AND BESS® is a registered trademark of Porgy And Bess Enterprises

Alfred

© 2009 Alfred Music Publishing Co., Inc.
All Rights Reserved. Printed in USA.

ISBN-10: 0-7390-6160-7
ISBN-13: 978-0-7390-6160-2

AIN'T MISBEHAVIN'

Alto Saxophone

Track 2: Full Performance
Track 3: Accompaniment

Music by
THOMAS "FATS" WALLER and HARRY BROOKS
Arranged by CARL STROMMEN

AS TIME GOES BY

Words and Music by
HERMAN HUPFELD
Arranged by CARL STROMMEN

Track 4: Full Performance
Track 5: Accompaniment

rit.

BUT NOT FOR ME

Music and Lyrics by
GEORGE GERSHWIN and IRA GERSHWIN
Arranged by CARL STROMMEN

Track 6: Full Performance
Track 7: Accompaniment

EMBRACEABLE YOU

Music and Lyrics by
GEORGE GERSHWIN and IRA GERSHWIN
Arranged by CARL STROMMEN

Track 8: Full Performance
Track 9: Accompaniment

I GOT RHYTHM

Music and Lyrics by
GEORGE GERSHWIN and IRA GERSHWIN
Arranged by CARL STROMMEN

Track 10: Full Performance
Track 11: Accompaniment

MY FUNNY VALENTINE

Music by
RICHARD RODGERS
Arranged by CARL STROMMEN

Track 12: **Full Performance**
Track 13: **Accompaniment**

OVER THE RAINBOW

Music by
HAROLD ARLEN
Arranged by CARL STROMMEN

Track 14: Full Performance
Track 15: Accompaniment

STRIKE UP THE BAND

Music and Lyrics by
GEORGE GERSHWIN and IRA GERSHWIN
Arranged by CARL STROMMEN

Track 16: Full Performance
Track 17: Accompaniment

SUMMERTIME

From "Porgy and Bess"®

Track 18: Full Performance
Track 19: Accompaniment

Music and Lyrics by GEORGE GERSHWIN,
DU BOSE and DOROTHY HEYWARD, and IRA GERSHWIN
Arranged by CARL STROMMEN

decresc.

p

SWEET GEORGIA BROWN

Words and Music by
BEN BERNIE, MACEO PINKARD and KENNETH CASEY
Arranged by CARL STROMMEN

Track 20: **Full Performance**
Track 21: **Accompaniment**

'S WONDERFUL

Music and Lyrics by
GEORGE GERSHWIN and IRA GERSHWIN
Arranged by CARL STROMMEN

Track 22: Full Performance
Track 23: Accompaniment

"Ain't Misbehavin'"

The music was written by Thomas "Fats" Waller and Harry Brooks. The words were written by Andy Razaf. It was first published in 1929. Waller was a pianist and composer, born in New York City in 1904 and died in Kansas City, Missouri in 1943. Brooks was also a pianist and composer born in Homestead, Pennsylvania in 1895 and died in Teaneck, New Jersey in 1970. The song was used in the musical theater productions of *Hot Chocolates* and *Ain't Misbehavin'*. It also was used in the films *Stormy Weather, You Were Meant for Me*, and *Gentlemen Marry Brunettes*. The melody was "borrowed" by Dmitri Shostakovich for the first movement of his Seventh Symphony. It was recorded by Ella Fitzgerald, Louis Armstrong, Miles Davis, Art Tatum, Sonny Stitt, Johnnie Ray, Sidney Bechet, Ray Charles, and Bill Haley & His Comets (who recorded a rock and roll version in 1957). In 1960, Tommy Bruce and the Bruisers had a #3 hit in the UK with their version of the song. Leon Redbone performed the song on "Saturday Night Live" in 1976. It served as the title song of the successful 1978 musical *Ain't Misbehavin'*. The original 1929 recording of "Ain't Misbehavin'" by Fats Waller received the Grammy Hall of Fame Award in 1984, and it was one of fifty recordings selected for inclusion in the National Recording Registry by the Library of Congress in 2004. In 2001, it was one of 365 Songs of the Century selected by the RIAA.

"As Time Goes By"

The words and music were written by Herman Hupfeld in 1931 for the Broadway musical *Everybody's Welcome*. He was a composer and lyricist, born in Montclair, New Jersey in 1894 and died there in 1951. The song became famous when it was featured in the Humphrey Bogart and Ingrid Bergman film *Casablanca*, which was released in 1942. It was also used in the musical film *She's Working Her Way Through College*, starring former president Ronald Reagan. The song was voted #2 on the AFI's *100 Years...100 Songs* special, commemorating the best songs in film. The song was also played by Clint Eastwood in the movie *In the Line of Fire*. The song's famous opening line, "You must remember this...," is actually the start of the fourth verse. As originally written and performed, there are three preceding verses. However, only the fourth verse was sung in *Casablanca*, and these are the lyrics that are well known today. It has been recorded by Barbra Streisand, Kenny Rogers, and Kenny G, and it was performed by "American Idol" finalist John Stevens in season three, 2004.

"But Not For Me," "Embraceable You," "I Got Rhythm," "Strike Up the Band," "Summertime"

George Gershwin was born in Brooklyn, New York on September 26, 1898. His parents emigrated from Russia in the early 1890s. He studied conventional piano technique and European classical music. At the age of 15, he became a "song plugger" for Jerome H. Remick and Company, a New York publishing firm. In 1916, he started working for Aeolian Company and Standard Music Rolls in New York, recording and arranging (under various pseudonyms) hundreds of player piano rolls. His first published song at the age of 17 earned him $5.00. His first hit song was "Swanee," published in 1919. In 1924, he and his older brother Ira (December 6, 1896–August 17, 1983) collaborated on a musical comedy called *Lady Be Good*. In 1927, they wrote the show *Strike Up the Band*, as well as *Funny Face* (included "'S Wonderful"), and in 1930 they came out with *Girl Crazy*, which included "I Got Rhythm," "Embraceable You," and "But Not for Me." In 1931, their show *Of Thee I Sing* won a Pulitzer Prize. In 1924, George composed his first classical work, *Rhapsody in Blue*™. It was premiered by the Paul Whiteman orchestra, and it is considered his finest work. His most ambitious composition was *Porgy and Bess*®, a "folk opera" in 1935 (included "Summertime"). George Gershwin died on July 11, 1937 in Beverly Hills, California at the age of 38.

"My Funny Valentine"

Richard Rodgers was born on June 28, 1902 in Queens, New York City. He started composing songs at summer camp in Maine. He attended Columbia University, but transferred to the Institute of Musical Art (now Juilliard). In 1919, he met Lorenz Hart (May 2, 1895–November 22, 1943), who also attended Columbia. They collaborated on many songs and shows, but did not get recognition until 1925 with *The Garrick Gaieties*, written for a benefit show for the Theatre Guild. It was only supposed to run one night, but re-opened and ran for 161 performances. They went on to write several hit shows for Broadway and London. In 1937, their show *Babes in Arms*, including "My Funny Valentine," ran for 289 performances at the Shubert Theatre. Later, the song was used in the musical films *Gentlemen Marry Brunettes* and *Pal Joey*, starring Frank Sinatra, Rita Hayworth, and Kim Novak. Rodgers went on to collaborate with Oscar Hammerstein II in the well-known musicals *Oklahoma!, Carousel, South Pacific, The King and I*, and *The Sound of Music*. Richard Rodgers died on December 30, 1979. He is only one of two persons (Marvin Hamlisch is the other) to have won an Oscar, an Emmy, a Tony Award, and a Pulitzer Prize.

"Over the Rainbow"

With music by Harold Arlen and lyrics by E. Y. Harburg, this song from the film, *The Wizard of Oz*, was voted the number one song of the twentieth century by the Recording Industry Association of America. Harold Arlen was born Chaim Arlook on February 15, 1905 in Buffalo, New York. He learned to play the piano, started a band as a young man, and in his early 20s moved to New York City, where he changed his name. He accompanied vaudeville acts and sang on recordings for many years. His first hit song, "Get Happy," was in collaboration with lyricist Ted Koehler in 1929. They wrote a number of hit songs, including "Let's Fall in Love" and "Stormy Weather." In writing for movie musicals in California, Arlen met E. Y. "Yip" Harburg (April 8, 1896–March 4, 1981). Their collaboration on *The Wizard of Oz* won them the Academy Award for Best Music, as well as Original Song. "Over the Rainbow" became Judy Garland's theme song after she sang it in the movie. Ironically, the song was cut three times from the final print of the movie because the publisher objected to the initial octave leap in the melody, but it was finally reinstated.

"Sweet Georgia Brown"

Written in 1925 by Ben Bernie, Maceo Pinkard, and Kenneth Casey, this song has become a jazz standard and well-known pop tune. Ben Bernie (b. May 30, 1891, Bayonne, New Jersey–d. October 23, 1943, Flushing, Queens County, New York) was an American jazz violinist and radio personality. His radio variety show was known has "Ben Bernie, The Old Maestro." His nationally known big band, Ben Bernie & His Hotel Roosevelt Orchestra, first recorded this song in 1926, and it became a five-week number one hit. It was at this time that he was added to the writing credits. Maceo Pinkard (b. June 27, 1897 in Bluefield, West Virginia–d. July 21, 1962 in New York City) was an American composer, lyricist, and music publisher. He was inducted into the National Academy of Popular Music "Songwriters Hall of Fame" in 1984. Kenneth Casey (b. January10, 1899, New York City–d. August 10, 1965, Cornwall, New York) was an American composer, publisher, author, and child actor. He acted in 50 films from 1909 to 1920. "Sweet Georgia Brown" is now known world-wide as the theme song of the basketball team, the Harlem Globetrotters.